Space, Time, and Loneliness

(A poetry chapbook)

E. Hughes

Love-LovePublishing, Madison, WI
Paperback ISBN: 978-1-961823-33-4
eBook ISBN: 978-1-961823-34-1
Space, Time, and Loneliness
Author: E. Hughes
Available formats: eBook | Paperback distribution

Dedication

To Brandon, Bishop, Alyssa, Blake, my husband Byron, and my
grandchildren Leon and Soul my eternal love, always.
To God, my Father in heaven:
Thank you for giving me a life worth living.

To my future grandchildren whom I have yet to meet,
I hope to become your eternal starlight in times of need.
Light-speed.

Other Works by E. Hughes

Fiction:

Sixth Iteration
Disappear, Love
Business as Usual
Infatuation
A Mediterranean Romance: The Capa Royals
The Sapphire Chronicles: Broken Lair
Hello (A Screenplay)
Pearls...

Nonfiction

Time and the Multi-Universe: A philosophy of time and time travel
Starting Your First Patio Garden: A Coffee Book
Family in a Time of Covid-19: The Truth about Coronavirus,
How to Protect Yourself and Prepare
Beyond the Plain (Poetry)
Reality Unbound: The Digital Mind (and the nature of reality) 2024
Space, Time, and Loneliness (A poetry chapbook)

Children's Books:

Penelope Helps Mom and Dad
Penelope: Super Duper Spectacular Princess Ballerina
Penelope: Be Kind to Animals
Penelope: Don't be afraid
Penelope Holiday Cheer
Garden of Secrets
2020 AD

Table of Contents

A cipher... to decipher...

"25181515181213261892287326197 264 148 845 541521245 97 339 58292786 2894. 71922 2327225447 2266 437 2211167 146."

422 831 3462 94 2698 6934 339 8 27316 2554. 5347 647 2645 15486 97.

Sometimes I Weep...

In the quiet hours, I sometimes weep,
in the wakeful silence, of counting sheep,
Everlasting love, I cannot keep,
In the quiet hours, I sometimes weep...

A fading silhouette, in heavenly light
The ethereal darkness, of my lost sight,
A waning glow, in morning's night,

Eternal sunshine, I dare not seek,
Deep in the shadows, I sometimes weep...

Sometimes I weep, in morning's night,
Where eternal love, burns deep and bright,
wingless limbs, that do take flight.

Your love-smile wilting, as I fade to sleep,
The ache of regret, where your warm heart beats,
In the quiet hours, I sometimes weep....

I Wish You Love

I wish you joy
I wish you love
I wish you *peace,*
and all of the above.
a slice of heaven,
and paradise, thereof,
I wish you courage,
I wish you love.

I wish you meadows and sparkling springs,
I wish you so many good and wonderful things,
I wish you the hope, of eternal streams,
I wish you an infinity, of realized dreams,
I wish you kindness. A million sunsets.
A million sunrises, and few regrets.

I wish you joy,
I wish you light,
the bliss of twinkling stars,
on a warm summer's night.
I wish you all,
In which you delight.
I wish you happiness,
and all of the above,
A slice of heaven,
and paradise, thereof,
I wish you, eternity,
I wish you love....

In the Land of the Lonely

In the land of the lonely
we hide our scars.
and bury our pain
in broken jars.
The cuts and bruises
never heal,
so we learn to suppress
the pain we feel.
In the land of the lonely,
there is nothingness
but the heavy burden
of silence.
In the land of the lonely
I feel so numb.
So I'll just lie here,
until I succumb.
I am invisible
so *no* one will care...
as I lurk in the shadows
of my despair.
In the land of the lonely,
We exist without friend.
We live on the outside
peering in.
In the land of the lonely
We hide our scars
until we fade away
like dying stars.

Have You Ever Felt Pain?

Have you ever felt
the death of a thousand suns?
or pain so great
that it weighed a ton?
Have you ever disappeared
without a trace?
As if flung from a void,
into outer space?
Have you ever felt pain so deep,
that you couldn't run?
Have you ever felt the death
of a thousand suns?
Yes, a common refrain
but have you ever, truly,
felt such pain?
That every moment of existence
fills you with dread?
That you feel that you are better
off dead?
Have you ever stood
in the morning light?
With pain so deep
it was as dark as night?
That you could grab the darkness
and swallow it whole?
And let the sadness,
consume your soul?
Have you ever felt the pain,
of a thousand suns?
Or pain so great,
That it weighed a ton?

The Burden of Pain

Pain is a burden
so we bury it deep
we drag it to bed
and nurse it to sleep.
When we open our eyes
we begin to weep.
Pain is a burden
we bury deep.

We lock it away in a chamber
with the secrets we keep
somewhere in our hearts
buried deep.
Where it grows and it grows
into a giant heap.
Pain is a burden
we bury deep.

It engulfs us in misery
even as we reap...
in the end,
I suppose I'll leap.
Because pain is a burden
We bury deep.

The Other Side

The scale of the universe
is incomprehensible to humankind
until it emerged
from the recesses of my mind
I escaped into the ethers of the universe,
one without time
left my body
and reality behind.
Plummeted into a black hole
and emerged on the other side.
Unconsciously conscious
of the conscious mind
awake and floating through space
to a *universe* without time
a dream within a dream
that left reality behind.
A dreamscape of a million suns,
planets, and stars combined
I merge into nothingness
on the other side.

Singularity

In the *beginning*
life is an endless tunnel
one seemingly without time
that stretches into the unknown
an equation of endless possibilities and light
becomes formless and dark
as we march into the night
of the unknown...shrinking into
oblivion
a tunnel that grows infinitely smaller
as we approach light speed
into deeper unknowns
where the tunnel ends
in a point of singularity.

My Third Eye Open

I **h**ave *no* poli**t**ic stance to take.
No political decisions I need **t**o make.
I am awake.
W**h**at differences does it mak**e**?
My third eye is open.

The ill**u**sion of choice.
A soundle**s**s voice.
The mental coercion
subversion.
Cannot suppress my **a**version.
My third eye open.

Who rule**$** the world?
When rulers are all the same
$ix degree$ of separation
$ix degree$ of a name.
We are just pawns in their game.
My third eye is open.

I am awake.
What difference does it make?
In the days and hours,
the lust for power.
Devour...
Us.
Who can *we* trust?
My third eye open.

The Force of Hate

Hate is a force
like a river on course
shaping and molding
injurious and scolding
a rhythmic percussion
a violent concussion
unwanted discussion.
Desperate to escape
drowning in hate
obliterate and bite
evisceration of light
ignorant and blind
not of sound mind
sick and contagious
confrontational and outrageous
a dangerous ploy
to seek and destroy
wicked and obscene
vicious and mean
impatient and annoyed
a soulless void
envious and mad
desperate and sad
empty and silent
fraught and violent.
Hate is a force
like a river on course.
Obsession of skin.
is death from within.

Present Illusions

When was now?
A second ago.
Time moves forward,
but where does it flow?
When was now?
A second ago.
Is it the past?
I do not know.
What a relentless,
persistent state,
it never ceases
to make me wait.
Is it the future?
I do not know.
Time moves forward.
But where does it flow?
Is it a ghost, a specter, *or* spook?
This is a notion, I must rebuke.
Is the future, the present
and the present, the past?
That's a question, I dare not ask.
When was now?
A second ago.
Is it the present?
I do not know.

I Pray We Meet Again

I say goodbye to the life I knew,
whisper goodbye to all of my friends,
as I bid our love adieu,
with a prayer that we'll meet again.
I pray we meet in the sunshine,
I pray we meet in the rain,
I pray we meet in the springtime,
In a meadow that never ends.
I pray our meeting is beautiful,
that our love can begin anew,
I say goodbye to my loving family,
with a promise to return to you.

Let us meet in a future life,
it matters not how or when,
my love is unbound by time or space,
I pray we meet again.

I can part with material things,
I can part with the life I knew,
I can part with my material self,
but I cannot part with you.

I pray our meeting is beautiful,
that our love can begin anew,
I say goodbye to my family,
with love I cannot subdue.

Let us meet in a future life,
it matters not how or when,
my love is unbound by time or space,
I pray we meet again.

Only the Lonely

Is there any situation that has made me feel lonelier
than misunderstanding the relationships in my life?
A miscalculation of my standing
in the hearts and minds of the people whom I have loved.
Only the lonely understand.

Is there anything that *has* made me feel lonelier,
than the perception of myself mirrored in the eyes of another?
The cold indifference.
The shallow disinterested gaze.
I blamed my own vanity for expecting more than I deserved.
Only the lonely understand.

Nothing ever made me feel lonelier
than a room full of people.
Only the lonely understand.

Prison of Solitude

I have too many secrets.
A prisoner of my own mind...
My prison a fortress of solitude.
That left me idled and confined.
I am isolated by my fears.
My truth is often blind.
Escaping a world I cannot control
    A world I can**n**ot **d**efine.
        The world from my small window
          Free to leave me behind.
            Lest I face, an open *space*
              Where the world
                is not too unkind.

The Impermanence of Being

I've come to understand much about impermanence.
The time I've borrowed from this *life.*
This temporary state of being.
So much meaning
given to that which has so little meaning
I face the inevitability of nonexistence.
That one day I will fade into the abyss of time.
I am an illusion
a fragile and yielding
cloud of trembling molecules
in an indifferent universe,
a creation of its boredom.
Each tear silent
laughter and joy that resounds
and echoes in a wave
of eternal starlight,
that spans through time and space, forever.

In the End

In the end was my beginning.
I existed for a frame of time.
Existed in matter and spirit.
I existed in conscious mind.

I leave you only memories of me...
That will fade from light to dark
As I leave this place, for open space
with the vibrations of your heart.
Echoes of me will remain here
in the spaces where we once stood
places filled with love and cheer,
carved in stone and wood.

In the end was my beginning
I return from whence I came
I existed only in conscious mind
to become a forgotten name.

Hunger

We live in a world,
that brings hunger to a child,
between the hugs and comfort
and a parent's weakened smiles.
What is hunger to a child,
but never-ending pain
and a burdened mother,
unable to explain?
What is hunger to a child,
but heartache and sadness,
that drives the mind
to desperation and madness?
What is hunger to a child,
but delirium and delusion,
despair and hope,
and sometimes confusion,
What is hunger to a child,
but torture and sorrow,
grasping for another day,
with no hope of tomorrow?
What is hunger to a child,
but suffering and need
in a world of abundance
but so full of greed?
What is hunger to a child,
in need of a caring hand,
what is hunger to a child,
unable to understand?

Thank You.

Thank you for the laughter,
thank you for the love you gave,
thank you for the smiles,
even when times were grave.
Thank you for your wisdom,
when I needed to be saved,
thank you for your strength,
in moments when I was less than brave.
Thank you for sparing me the sadness
of sorrowful goodbyes,
for pretending to be cheerful,
even with tears in your eyes.
Thank you for the laughter,
for your kindness through years of pain,
thank you for enduring me,
even when I complained.
Thank you for showing me the light,
for your tenderness and care,
for being patient with me,
when I ranted that life wasn't fair.
Thank you for granting me,
a space to be who I am,
for embracing my inner-tiger,
and for cradling my inner-lamb.
Thank you for the laughter,
thank you for the years,
thank you for your cheerful goodbyes,
and for your laughter through all of the tears.

The Love You Gave

The love you gave
meant the world to me
I will hold it close
for all eternity

The love you gave
filled me with hope
a beam of salvation
at the *end* of a rope.

The love you gave
was a home
that filled my heart
when I was alone.

The love you gave
kept me alive
the love you gave
helped me survive.

The love you gave
I held it close
it opened my heart
when I was morose.

The love you gave
taught me to forgive.
The love you gave,
is the reason I live.

An Infinite Destiny

In the midnight hour
under the crescent moon...
Forgive me—as I approach light speed
far too soon.
An infinite destiny,
that comes like a monsoon,
In the midnight hour,
under a quarter moon,
it spins like a clock,
around 'til noon,
stops in the midnight hour,
under a waning moon.
Forgive me—as I approach light speed
far too soon.
I have a date with destiny,
a date with time,
that spins round and round,
at two plus a dime.
Forgive me—as I approach light speed
far too soon.
In the midnight hour,
waning and waxing,
under a full moon.
Forgive me—as I approach light speed
far too soon.
It spins around like a clock,
under a new moon.

The Clearing

The day was cold, listless and dreary,
My poor body tired, broken, and weary. Shook off my slumber,
and set about on my way, into the deepest, greenest, gathering of
trees, where I might find shelter, from autumn's brutal and
frigid breeze.

My belly was empty, and yet I was full, my eyes glistening, like a
whirling vortex, of deep brown pools.
My vigilance heightened, into sharpened tools, until I heard the
snapping of a branch. My poor heart racing, and my face
blanched.

I spun about. What was there? But swaying trees and stagnant air?
I smiled quietly, and forged ahead, despite a feeling of doom, and a
sense of dread, as the chill of an evening breeze, nipped at my head.

Darkness descended much like a cloak. I felt a lump rise, at the back
of my throat. *What am I doing here? Why did I elope?* The woods
spun about, as I realized my error. I was quite lost, and suddenly in
terror. I searched my mind, for what this journey entailed, yet
uncertainty, and amnesia, only seemed to prevail.

A spooky tension, hung prominent in the air with a fleeting
moment of growing despair. *Who am I, and what am I doing
here?* I met a clearing, where I felt like prey. I was exposed, and
quite on display.
"Go back, go back, and be on your way!"
"Who goes there?" I cried, only two steps away. I stared into an
abyss, of towering trees, with bits of dark voids, between the
bushes and leaves.
"Go back! Go back! Now do as I say!"
But I am Here, perhaps I should pray?"

I was so startled that I trembled and seized, afraid of the abyss, the branches, and trees. I couldn't shake the feeling, I was so ill at ease.

I could not go back from whence I came, as I could not recall, a step, or a frame. My eyes swelled with tears; I openly wept. "Come out, come out, I demand you to show yourself."

The bushes shook, and the soil rumbled, I heard a grunt, and finally a grumble, "Leave this place, be on your way, or this will become, a most terrible day!" I was compelled, and surely went away. I walked and I walked, tired and fearing, but again I returned, to the same old clearing. What am I doing here? What shall I do? The voice then rumbled, "The end is in the beginning, so find something new!"

I walked and I walked, in a circle of dread, I walked and walked, with a lifetime in my head, I walked and I walked, a square mile instead, ' I saw geometric gathering, of bushes and trees, bowing and swaying in their own little groups, again, I arrived at the clearing, in an infinite loop, I walked and I walked, in a circle of dread, I walked and I walked, and longed for a bed, I walked and I walked, tired and fearing, And again I arrived, at the same dismal clearing, "I am so tired and saddened, oh what shall I do?" The voice then rumbled, "Time and space is but an infinite loop. The end is in the beginning so find something new!"

I walked and I walked, tired and fearing, but again I returned, to the same old clearing, with a feeling of doom and a sense of dread, when suddenly a thought, emerged in my head. Perhaps I am here, because I am dead? The voice then rumbled, "Time and space is but an infinite loop. The end is in the beginning so find something new!"

21

Bonus Story

Ten-Speed

A short story by E. Hughes

It was a ten-speed bike. I remember looking over my mother's shoulder to get a glimpse at the doorway of my father rolling it into the house. It was my sister's 12th birthday. I was excited by the prospect of owning a bike for the first time. Even though the bike was for Mia, we shared everything so it was as good as both of ours, anyway.

I was nine years-old but never learned to ride. Over the years, I was grateful to have owned a pair of roller-skates, so I never felt left out or as though a piece of my childhood was missing because I never owned a bike. When kids rode their bikes down the street I quickly grabbed my skates and took off after them. I'd grab a hold of of their seats as they peddled and let the bike pull me as fast as it could before I finally let go, skidding uncontrollably down the sidewalk or street. I had a blast. The skates were size-adjustable, metal, and fit around my shoes. If you were a kid in the eighties you probably owned a pair.

The wheels were metal and quite noisy. It produced a grinding sound—heavy steel scraping against uneven concrete that sometimes made you fall if you hit a bump too quickly. You sort of got used to band-aids over skinned-knees. I rode the skates hard, hoping they would spark when I hit the brakes or skid to a screeching halt. Sometimes, I'd take those loud metal skates outside as early as seven or eight in the morning and circle our city block wearing pigtails and a bright-colored bubble romper… the kind that you had to tie in bow at the top of each shoulder. They were thin and cotton. I had several of them in multiple colors so picking out my own clothes and racing outside was an easy task, especially in the morning before my mother woke up. Even then, at six or seven-years old I loved the quiet and stillness of the early hours and the sweet pungent smell of morning dew. I'd wake the neighbors skating around the block, but they let me be. It was the 1980s and still relatively safe, even in our slightly sketchy neighborhood.

A year before my sister was gifted the ten-speed bike I outgrew the loud metal skates and upgraded to the kind you'd find at a skating rink… ankle-high skates with pink wheels and laces on the front. They were light, which allowed me to incorporate fancy dance moves, maneuvers, and tricks into my skating routine. But getting a new bike raised the specter of my excitement significantly. My sister Mia was happy about the gift, though not as happy as I was.

Mia was a quiet sort of person who lacked the child-like exuberance I often exhibited. We had a working mother so we were latchkey kids who mostly took care of ourselves during the week. Mia had to be responsible for me when she was as young as seven years-old and had taken on a number of other household responsibilities unbefitting someone her age while our mother worked a job as a secretary. This gave Mia a level of maturity and gravity beyond her years at a very early age. While I was skating, playing double-dutch, break-dancing on broken-down cardboard boxes, exploring our neighborhood and alleyways in search of "dead bodies" or for animals with broken limbs, Mia was listening to Rick James, Michael Jackson, and Paul McCartney on our record player and thinking about boys. She'd always been that way. So while getting a bike was fun, she wasn't as interested as I was… just mildly amused by my excitement. Seeing me happy made her smile.

As soon as our father drove away we took the bike outside. Neither one of us could ride so we taught ourselves, getting on, and falling sideways…trying to peddle and keep from tipping over. We'd make it a little further each try, taking turns…me, waiting impatiently every time Mia got on the bike. We'd go back inside for the night with scrapes on our ankles and knees from falling over or getting raked by the sharp metal ridges lining the pedals. However, by the end of summer, we both had sufficiently managed to conquer the bike. By then, the ten-speed was in awful shape. The chain would come off or snap mid-ride, causing us to fall. The spokes in the wheel were bent and dented. Too many falls had badly damaged it. This was not a huge concern. My birthday was a few months away and another bike would be coming our way. We'd treat that one better, especially since we both knew how to ride. The first ten-speed was "on-the-job" learning experience.

Me and my sister knew how to share with each other because we learned at an early age and shared almost everything our entire lives. Of course, there were many ups and downs, as well as cat-fights, but in the end there was always a sense of loyalty. We understood how to look out for each other even if we were mad at each other. We even shared each other's deepest secrets, and for Mia, there were many. I don't think a day went by during my childhood that I ever disliked Mia. Perhaps because she always felt so grown-up…like someone who was more than a big sister to me.

Mia was also very pretty, which only added to her grownup charm. Because of this, she was wildly liked by family members…especially the family members on my father's side. They'd taken a special interest in Mia, interest that they'd never taken in me. Sometimes they'd stop by to pick her up and take her to family events or for regular visits with their families. My mother would allow her to go but the invitation to join them was rarely extended to me—so rarely, that when the invitation was finally extended because everyone on my father's side of the family was likely going, I usually declined out of a strong sense of pride. There were times when I ended up going anyway, usually because it was our weekend at my father's house. I hated family gatherings. Some of the adults—one in particular, was downright rude and made a point of letting me know that I wasn't welcome.

"Ursula!" she'd say in an agitated voice, calling me away from the other children. "Get your bald-headed raggedly butt over here and finish your food." My aunt Tippy was always looking for a reason to chastise me over something. And she never let me forget that I was too skinny for her liking. "With your bony, bald-headed butt!" she'd screech.

I'd do what was asked and get away from her as soon as possible. I was grateful the other aunts ignored me. They ignored me so much I couldn't keep their names straight because there had never been an opportunity to get to know them. They avoided eye contact or talking to me as much as possible. Mia noticed, but didn't understand why. Sometimes they'd make a fuss over the way I looked.

"Big-headed girl, she looks like Tweetie-Bird," one of the adults would laugh. Tippy would wait until the other adults weren't around, especially if my step-mother wasn't in the room before she'd make snide off-handed remarks that took the insults to another level. "With your ugly, self," she'd say. My stepmother was nice and seemed to like us, so Tippy would not have talked that way in front of her.

I had no idea what I'd done to rub his family the wrong way but they couldn't stand me, and I couldn't stand them. Did they think picking on me was funny? Did they do it to the other children? If they did, I didn't see it. For some reason it felt like I was always the target. But this had given me a quiet strength, a deep sense of pride and the ability to stand up for myself. Even though it hurt my feelings, their words didn't make me crumble. Being a family outcast taught me not to bend to authority or abusive voices. I hated ignorance of any kind. Thankfully, I didn't interact with them often. Between the rarely extended invitations and the fact that I carefully avoided them, I managed to escape any unwanted interactions.

Soon the school year would start and Mia and I eventually healed from the scrapes and bruises we endured from the bike over the summer. I was looking forward to October. My birthday couldn't come soon enough. I didn't talk to my father often. In fact, I can barely remember having a five minute conversation with him. Our weekends at his house were mostly spent with our stepmother and younger sister. He was always out until late night hours and when he came home we were already asleep. I didn't pretend to understand the nuances of their relationship and I never questioned why he did certain things. For us—he was a bit of a legend...a hero when we compared him to our mother. He was a likeable man—an entertainer with a lot of friends and people around him. His laid-back personality was very similar to Mia's. But he was also a secretive, distant, sort of person, and not at all mature in the ways that Mia was. But perhaps I felt that way because I never got to know him.

It wasn't long before October rolled around along with my birthday. Mia always had great birthdays but mine were always met with misfortune...perhaps because it was so close to Halloween. I was jinxed!

The year before was a bit of a disaster when my mother lost her wallet along with the money she had saved for my birthday cake and presents. So instead of celebrating my birthday we went to visit her sister. I spent the entire day putting on a brave face. With weak half-smiles meant to make everyone feel better, I hoped no one noticed the tears swelling in my eyes when they looked away. The dam finally broke when a cousin mocked the bag of Halloween candy her mother had given us as we sat on the floor with our legs folded watching, It's the Great Pumpkin, Charlie Brown. The cousin had leaned towards me and cackled, "Is this all you're getting for your birthday?" knowing full well we didn't have any money to celebrate.

As I burst into tears, my aunt's instant reaction was to slap her across the face for making fun of me. This was a sensitive subject in the family that day. We were all trying to tip-toe around it and hearing the words out loud was like ripping open a gaping emotional wound. And while the lost wallet was an accident, I still managed to feel like no one cared about me—I felt overlooked. Why did it always happen on my birthday? Still, I felt guilty for resenting how my birthday turned out that year. My mother was miserable and angry with herself so I dusted myself off and put on a brave face for her. The end of the month was always rough for us and she honestly tried her best to keep us fed and with a roof over our heads. Naturally, my father didn't show up or have anything to offer—not even a happy birthday wish, which would have made my dismal day much brighter. I'm not even sure if he knew it was my birthday. But since he'd shown up with a bike for Mia earlier that year, I was certain this birthday would also be different for me.

Thankfully the day met all of my expectations. Even though finances were tight, there was birthday cake and birthday presents. No party, we rarely did those. Mama disliked company so we celebrated with my brother and Mia just as I had anticipated. It was a low-key affair.

I'd gotten a new Sweet Valley High book, a Barbie, and a She-Ra castle. Still, I watched the clock and listened for the doorbell all day—occasionally running to the window hoping to see my father unloading a bike from the trunk of his car. I waited and I waited as the hours ticked by and soon, noon turned to dusk, and dusk to night. I eventually went to bed sulking and disappointed, yet not in the least bit surprised. A feeling of loneliness and isolation washed over me as I lay in bed gazing at the window, still hoping.

When hadn't these people disappointed me? Over the years I chalked it up to "middle-child syndrome" but even that didn't seem a good enough reason for my family's indifference.

My mother and father split while she was still pregnant with me. He'd left her for another woman. I was in the precarious place of connecting two people who no longer wanted to be together while Mia had the privilege of being the oldest—the first born, the first to do everything. She had the privilege of being a child conceived out of love and I had the privilege of not being wanted. Pretty much anything I did after Mia wasn't really of interest to anyone because I was tacked on at the end of a dying relationship.

A few years later my father and stepmother had a child of their own. She was their baby...the youngest. A cute little jelly-bean. I adored her.

Eventually my mother moved on to a new relationship too. It didn't last long, but she had a son—and he was her pride and joy. Her baby. Sadly, she was a woman who favored male children and exhibited feelings of derision and hostility towards her daughters, so Mia and I learned to rely on each other for emotional and mental support. I slowly began to understand why Mia was so mature and aged beyond her years as I started to see patterns in our family I didn't notice before.

In the end I learned a valuable lesson from the bike...the first of which was not to expect anything from anyone. People can't disappoint you if you don't expect anything from them in the first place. I never received a present, a card, or acknowledgement from my father that year, or any other year thereafter and I was at peace with that. I decided if he didn't extend the opportunity to have a conversation or a relationship with me then I would not extend the opportunity to him.

So we rarely spoke over the years...unless we absolutely needed to, and eventually, we no longer needed to. He maintained a close relationship with Mia and his other children and I moved forward in life, content with the unspoken solitude and mutual distance between us. But it became the template for how I would handle other relationships in my life. The bar I set was high. I had to feel like I was special to someone. I never fully understood why I was different from the other children and as much as I wanted answers from family members I knew I would never get them. Eventually, my relationship with all of these people would fade until we became strangers...no harsh words spoken or sad goodbyes... There's an outcast in every family and I just happened to be the outcast in mine.

I eventually met the man who would become my husband, a person who made an effort to make every birthday special. As the matriarch of our family, when I had children, birthdays were always a big deal in our house. There was always a celebration where everyone was cherished and no one felt left out or forgotten.

About the Author

E. Hughes is a novelist and writer of more than twenty-five years and has over twenty published books in multiple genres from fiction novels, nonfiction works, poetry, and children's books to date. Her first book of poetry, "*Beyond the Plain*" was published in 2003. Her second collection of poetry, "*Digital Smiles*" was released in 2024, with her collection of unreleased poetry in *Space, Time, and Loneliness*, released shortly after. Hughes is also the author of *Time and the Multi-Universe: a philosophy of time and time travel*, *Reality Unbound: The Digital Mind (and the nature of reality)* and the novel, *Sixth Iteration*.

www.ingramcontent.com/pod-product-compliance
Lightning Source LLC
Chambersburg PA
CBHW051010140626
46546CB00016B/1701